This book is a gift

To:

"Cheryl!"

From:

Your friend Linda

Date:

December 2002

Message:

Given prayfully & lovingly to you, my special friend!

31 VALUES FOR LIFE

GOLDEN THOUGHTS

Murray Janson

Christian Art Gifts

Originally published by Christelike Uitgewers-
maatskappy under the title *Goue gedagtes*

English edition published by Christian Art Gifts,
PO Box 1599, Vereeniging 1930, South Africa

Designed by Christian Art Gifts

Translated by Haidee Kotze

Printed in Singapore

ISBN 1-86852-768-9

01 02 03 04 05 06 07 08 09 10 - 10 9 8 7 6 5 4 3 2 1

Golden Thoughts

- Day -

1

These are the words of him who is holy and true, who holds the key of David. What he opens no one can shut, and what he shuts no one can open ... See, I have placed before you an open door that no one can shut.
(Revelation 3:7-8)

New Year's resolutions? Less talking and more doing;
less complaints and more acceptance;
less wounding and more giving;
less for myself and more for my spouse;
more sensitivity and more service;
less theology and more prayer.

A prayer for the new year? Lord, let your image be ever more clearly expressed in my life and doings.

- DAY -

2

*Now is your time of grief,
but I will see you again and
you will rejoice, and no one
will take away your joy.
(John 16:22)*

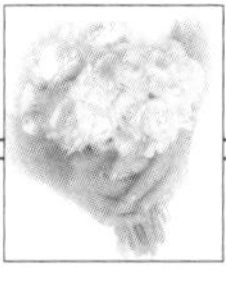

Cheerfulness is having sufficient courage in the Lord to be joyful, and therefore also having sufficient joy in the Lord to be of good courage.

There is no greater comfort or joy to be found than the certain knowledge that you are enveloped by love even when you are surrounded by fear and distress.
(John Calvin)

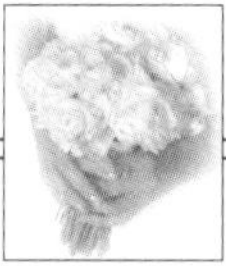

- Day -

3

Friend, your sins are forgiven.
(Luke 5:20)

Come and share your
master's happiness!
(Matthew 25:21)

To him who is thirsty I will
give to drink without cost from
the spring of the water of life.
(Revelation 21:6)

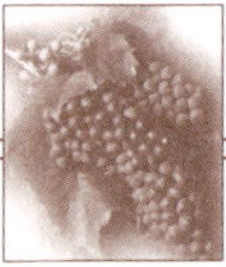

The eyes of people tie me to my past, but the gaze of Jesus opens a new future before me.

I try not to look too far ahead or too far back – but I always look up.
(Charlotte Brontë)

I look up, and I have faith …
(Dr. W. A. Hofmeyr)

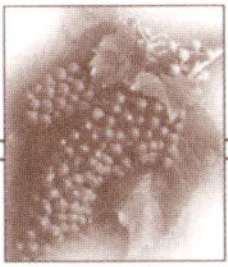

- Day -

4

Therefore go and make disciples of all nations, baptising them in the name of the Father and of the Son and of the Holy Spirit, and teaching them to obey everything I have commanded you. (Matthew 28:19-20)

Don't allow your joy to be dependent upon your circumstances. Your joy should come from God himself, who is with you at all times and in all circumstances.

I know that there is nothing better for men than to be happy and do good while they live. That everyone may … find satisfaction in all his toil – this is the gift of God. (Ecclesiastes 3:12-13)

- Day -

5

Everything is possible
for him who believes.
(Mark 9:23)

Blessed are those
who have not seen
and yet have believed.
(John 20:29)

Don't be afraid; just believe.
(Mark 5:36)

Faith is there to be used. He who does not need it, will not receive it.

Faith can change any direction, light any path, and alleviate all misery. It transforms sorrow into joy, tension into peace, animosity into friendship, and hell into heaven. Faith is God at work.
(F. L. Holmes)

- Day -

6

But he who has been forgiven little loves little.
(Luke 7:47)

Through love and faithfulness sin is atoned for …
(Proverbs 16:6)

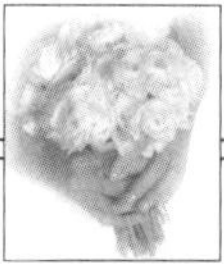

The extent of the human being's greatness is directly proportional to the extent of his love. It can cause a millionaire to shrink to the size of a dime, while causing a little mother to become as sublimely great as the world for which she prays.

God is love. This is simultaneously the most human and the most divine message of all time. (Phil Bosmans)

- DAY -

7

Some time later, Jesus went up to Jerusalem for a feast ...
(John 5:1)

... and he brought festivity and joy into the life of even the unhappiest person!

Do you seek joy? Kindle it in someone else's life, and soon your life will also be aglow with joy.

Accept every new day as a gift … Look in the mirror, smile at yourself, and say good morning to yourself. At the very least you will then already have had some practice in also showing the same kindness to others!
(Phil Bosmans)

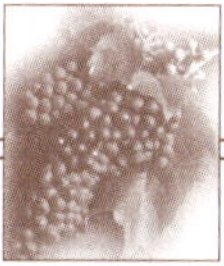

- Day -

8

Let your gentleness be evident to all … And the peace of God, which transcends all understanding, will guard your hearts and your minds in Christ Jesus. (Philippians 4:5-7)

In order to pass on one gram of bitterness to another person you need to produce dozens of kilograms of bitterness in your own heart. Therefore you should strive to produce joyfulness and good cheer instead.

May the Lord, the Maker of heaven and earth, bless you … (Psalm 134:3)

- Day -

9

Do to others as you would have them do to you. Love your enemies, do good to them … Then … you will be sons of the Most High …

(Luke 6:31, 35)

The colours that you use to paint with continue to cling to your hands. Therefore it is best, also for yourself, to paint others with the colours of joy.

I give back what has been given to me; where flowers were planted, flowers will burgeon.
(Jan F. E. Cilliers)

- Day -

10

Rejoice in the Lord always.
I will say it again: Rejoice!
(Philippians 4:4)

Even though you do not see
him now, you believe in him
and are filled with an
inexpressible and glorious joy.
(1 Peter 1:8)

In his letter to the Philippians Paul instructs them to rejoice in the Lord. He also tells them not to be anxious about anything, but to present all their requests and desires to God. In doing so they will have the prospect of receiving the peace of God, which transcends all understanding. What a glorious promise this is, and yet there are pitifully few people who follow these instructions as they should be followed. Do you?

- Day -

11

Here I am! I stand at the door and knock. If anyone hears my voice and opens the door, I will come in and eat with him, and he with me. (Revelation 3:20)

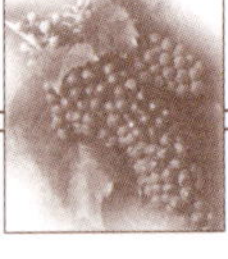

Very often our problem is that we pray to the Lord to come into our hearts and lives, and yet we refuse to give him permission to win us over completely for him and his kingdom. What good would it possibly do us to gain the whole world if we in so doing forfeit our souls? Give the Lord that indispensable permission to win you over for him!

- Day -

12

Love is … not self-seeking … It always protects, always trusts, always hopes, always perseveres. (1 Corinthians 13:4-5, 7)

The doors that lead to happiness only open to the outside.

A happy person brings light into the darkness of others' lives. He brings life where once was death. He does not indulge in his own problems, does not expect others to simply give him everything he wants, and accepts responsibility for his own life.
(Phil Bosmans)

- Day -

13

May I never boast except in the cross of our Lord Jesus Christ, through which the world has been crucified to me, and I to the world.
(Galatians 6:14)

After Simon of Cyrene had carried Jesus' cross for a brief time, Jesus' cross carried him ever after.

The cross brings you back to the truth ... It is like an antenna or aerial which helps you to receive the transmission of God's message.
(Phil Bosmans)

- Day -

14

She will give birth to a son, and you are to give him the name Jesus, because he will save his people from their sins. (Matthew 1:21)

God went so far as to allow the light of his Son's life to be extinguished, so that he could seek and find those who are lost.

I tell you the truth, unless a kernel of wheat falls to the ground and dies, it remains only a single seed. But if it dies, it produces many seeds.
(John 12:24)

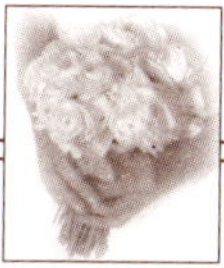

- Day -

15

He gave himself for us to redeem us from all wickedness and to purify for himself a people that are his very own, eager to do what is good.
(Titus 2:14)

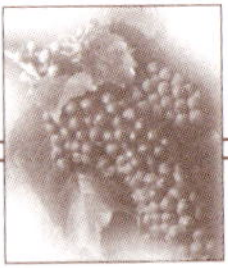

Christ died on the cross for *you personally* – as if you were the only person on earth. Therefore you too ought to become *personally* involved with someone who is in distress – as if he or she were the only person on earth. Ultimately this is the only way in which we can truly help one another.

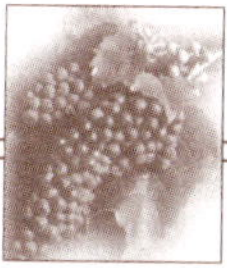

- Day -

16

He was delivered over to death for our sins and was raised to life for our justification. (Romans 4:25)

God's answer to his scorned and crucified love is Jesus, who was raised to life so that everyone's sins may be forgiven.

Love is not an invention of the human mind. It is God's gift of grace. It is God himself.

Without love our time here on earth becomes pure hell.
(St. Augustine of Hippo)

- Day -

17

Rejoice with those who rejoice; mourn with those who mourn. (Romans 12:15)

Happiness is not to *feel* happy, but to *make* happy.

Therefore my prayer will be: Lord, grant me a joyful spirit and a grateful heart, so that I may praise your name!

I look ahead, and I am courageous.
(Dr. W. A. Hofmeyr)

- Day -

18

Not everyone who says to me, "Lord, Lord," will enter the kingdom of heaven, but only he who does the will of my Father who is in heaven. (Matthew 7:21)

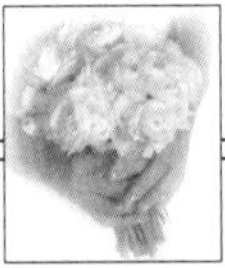

There comes a time when you have to abandon *your* principles and simply do what is right!

Grant me the knowledge that inspires me to surmount the mountains of ignorance, so that I, your creation devoted to serving only you, will be able to see the light of truth.
(C. Louis Leipoldt)

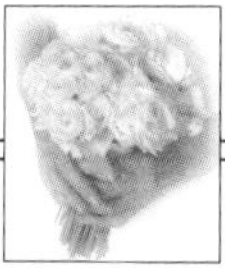

- Day -

19

For we are to God the aroma of Christ among those who are being saved and those who are perishing. (2 Corinthians 2:15)

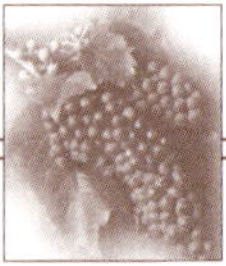

Joyfulness of spirit is not an unwavering state of mind, but a daily challenge.

Whatever is true, whatever is noble, whatever is right, whatever is pure, whatever is lovely, whatever is admirable – if anything is excellent or praiseworthy – think about such things.
(Philippians 4:8)

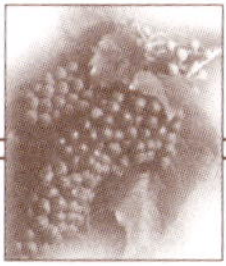

- Day -

20

If anyone says, "I love God," yet hates his brother, he is a liar. For anyone who does not love his brother, whom he has seen, cannot love God, whom he has not seen. (I John 4:20)

You can love God only as much as you love those whom you love the least.

You ought to love your neighbour as you love yourself ... Surely this also means that you should see in your neighbour that which God intended him or her to be?
(D. Moorrees)

Despite everything I continue to believe that love is more powerful than hatred.
(Annie van Niekerk)

- Day -

21

I will not leave you as orphans; I will come to you. Before long, the world will not see me anymore, but you will see me. Because I live, you also will live. (John 14:18-19)

Jesus ascended to heaven for the sole purpose of returning to and living in each and every one of us in the shape of his Holy Spirit.

The Holy Spirit, which is God's gift of grace, produces in us love for one another. And this love, which is perfect, drives all fear and selfishness from our hearts.

- Day -

22

But the fruit of the Spirit is
love, joy, peace, patience,
kindness, goodness,
faithfulness, gentleness
and self-control …
(Galatians 5:22-23)

We need not pursue worldly things in a (vain) attempt to find the source of true happiness. Every believer has the Holy Spirit in his or her heart, and the Spirit wishes to bring forth in us his fruit. And the fruit of the Spirit includes love and life and peace.

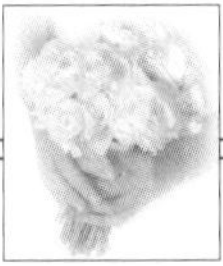

- DAY -

23

If I give all I possess to the poor and surrender my body to the flames, but have not love, I gain nothing.
(1 Corinthians 13:3)

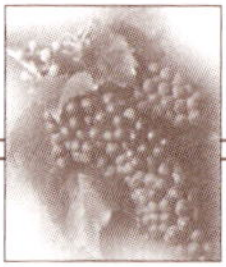

A thousand deeds without love will never be equal to one act of love.

Isn't this our greatest and even our only need – the need to be loved? And isn't this the only way in which we can truly help one another – by loving one another?
(Berta Smit)

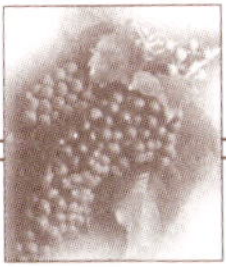

- Day -

24

Although he was a son, he learned obedience from what he suffered and, once made perfect, he became the source of eternal salvation for all who obey him.
(Hebrews 5:8-9)

Learning to understand what it is that God is trying to tell us through our suffering is much more important than being released from our suffering.

God sometimes speaks to us through hardship – or sometimes in spite thereof.
(Philip Yancey)

God comes to us and fills our sorrow with his presence.
(Paul Claudel)

- Day -

25

You stiff-necked people, with uncircumcised hearts and ears! You are just like your fathers: You always resist the Holy Spirit!

(Acts 7:51)

God's voice and his love resonate like the sea all around us, but we continue to resist him as dikes resist the sea.

How great is the heart that finds in itself that divine order which makes all life's vicissitudes cohere in ultimate unity!
(C. M. van den Heever)

- Day -

26

The watchman … calls his own sheep by name and leads them out. When he has brought out all his own, he goes on ahead of them, and his sheep follow him because they know his voice.
(John 10:3-4)

Christians do not follow the Lord as carriages follow a locomotive, but rather as sheep follow their shepherd.

So many people seek happiness in places where they, sadly, will never find it. Only the soul which has been cleansed and purified by the blood of Christ and which shares in the peace of God, can know and experience true happiness.

(A Christian)

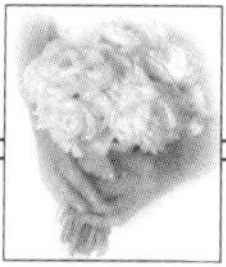

- DAY -

27

I will lie down and sleep in peace, for you alone, O Lord, make me dwell in safety.
(Psalm 4:8)

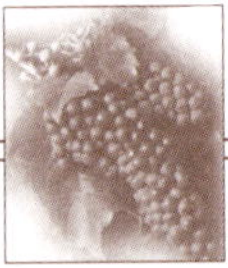

Why would you allow your problems to keep you awake at night? Give them to the Lord – after all, he is awake in any case.

He who watches over you will not slumber; indeed, he who watches over Israel will neither slumber nor sleep. The Lord watches over you …
(Psalm 121:3-5)

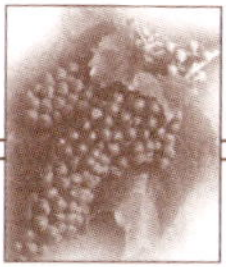

- Day -

28

I cry aloud to the Lord; I lift up my voice to the Lord for mercy. I pour out my complaint before him; before him I tell my trouble. (Psalm 142:1-2)

If I had to talk only *about* God I would never have been able to have faith in him, but now I can also talk *to* him.
(Martin Buber)

God warms his hands at man's heart whenever he prays.
(John Masefield)

To pray is to keep silent … until you hear God's voice.
(Sören Kierkegaard)

- Day -

29

All day long I have held out my hands to an obstinate people, who walk in ways not good, pursuing their own imaginations …
(Isaiah 65:2)

There is infinite peace to be found in the knowledge that God never leaves us in peace to follow our own minds.

O God, you have made us to be yours, and we will never find peace until we have found it in you.
(St. Augustine of Hippo)

He makes me lie down in green pastures, he leads me beside quiet waters.
(Psalm 23:2)

- Day -

30

In the same way, let your light shine before men, that they may see your good deeds and praise your Father in heaven. (Matthew 5:16)

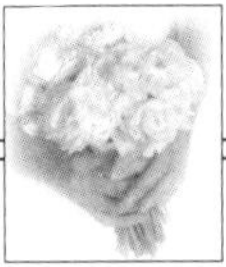

Our cats and dogs must be able to see that we are Christians who regularly attend church.
(Martin Luther)

If I am not a Christian in my marriage then I am not a Christian anywhere, even though I might believe that I am a Christian everywhere.

... a great deal of tolerance, many good deeds, and infinite forgiveness.
(Antoon Lavater)

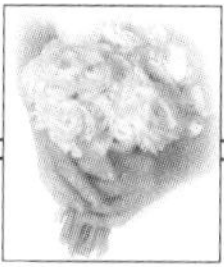

- Day -

31

Neither death nor life,
neither angels nor demons,
neither the present nor
the future, nor any powers ...
... will be able to separate us
from the love of God that
is in Christ Jesus our Lord.
(Romans 8:38-39)

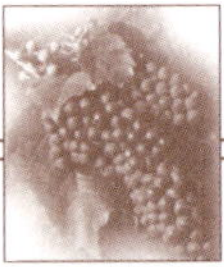

Jesus Christ is the exclamation mark after the words "God is love!"

"God is love!" our hearts rejoice, and when we ponder the true nature of love we begin to understand that it is epitomised in the fact that God sent his son to die on the cross so that our sins may be forgiven.

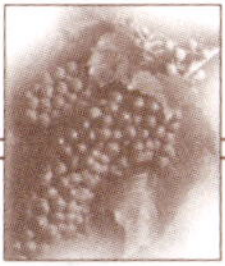